Finding Inspiration

Cultivating Creativity and Innovation

Rabeal Daudpota

Acknowledgment

Writing a book is never a solitary task, and I am incredibly grateful to the many people who have supported me throughout this journey. First and foremost, I want to thank my family for their unwavering love and encouragement, which has kept me going through the ups and downs of this process. Thank you for believing in my vision and for helping me to bring it to fruition.

I would also like to express my gratitude to the many friends and colleagues who have provided invaluable support and inspiration along the way. Your encouragement, advice, and feedback have been instrumental in making this book a reality, and I am deeply grateful for your friendship and generosity.

Finally, I want to thank my readers, whose interest and enthusiasm for my work have been a constant source of motivation and inspiration. Without you, this book would not exist, and I am honored and humbled by your support.

Thank you all for being a part of this journey with me.

Dedication

This book is dedicated to my family members and friends, who have been my constant source of love, support, and inspiration.

Thank you for always being there for me, for listening to my ideas, and for providing me with the space and time I needed to write. Your love and support have been a constant source of strength and motivation, and I am forever grateful for the role you have played in shaping me into the writer I am today.

Table of Contents

Overview of the Book's Purpose and Structure

The purpose of the book ***"Finding Inspiration: Cultivating Creativity and Innovation"*** is to provide readers with practical tools and strategies for developing their creative and innovative skills in both personal and professional contexts. The book is designed to help readers overcome common obstacles to creativity and innovation, such as fear, self-doubt, and lack of motivation, and to cultivate a mindset that is open to new ideas and approaches.

The book is divided into three main sections. The first section of the book, **"Understanding Creativity and Innovation,"** provides a comprehensive overview of the concept of creativity and innovation, with their examples. It moves forward into different forms, benefits, and obstacles that might hinder the creative process.

The section begins with a clear definition of creativity and its different forms, such as artistic creativity, problem-solving creativity, and scientific creativity. It further explores the nature of creative thinking and the importance of divergent thinking, which involves generating multiple solutions to a problem.

The section then delves into the benefits of creativity and innovation in personal and professional life. It discusses how creativity and innovation can enhance personal growth and development, lead to greater job satisfaction, and improve organizational performance. It also highlights the importance of creativity and innovation in driving economic growth and social development.

However, creativity and innovation can be hindered by various obstacles such as fear, self-doubt, lack of motivation, and limited thinking patterns. The section identifies these obstacles and provides practical strategies to overcome them. For example, it suggests adopting a growth mindset that emphasizes learning and development, practicing mindfulness to increase focus and creativity, and seeking out diverse experiences to expand perspectives.

Overall, the "Understanding Creativity and Innovation" section sets the foundation for the rest of the book by providing readers with a clear understanding of the nature and benefits of creativity and the common obstacles that might hinder the creative process. By cultivating this understanding, readers are better equipped to develop their creative and innovative skills and apply them in their personal and professional lives.

The second section of the book, **"Cultivating Creativity and Innovation,"** is dedicated to providing readers with practical tools and strategies for developing their creativity and innovation skills.

This section begins by exploring the common obstacles to creativity and innovation, such as fear, self-doubt, and a lack of motivation. It then provides practical exercises and activities designed to help readers overcome these obstacles and cultivate a mindset that is open to new ideas and approaches.

For example, the section may provide exercises that encourage readers to think outside of their comfort zone, such as brainstorming sessions where readers are encouraged to generate as many ideas as possible without judgment. Other activities may focus on increasing self-awareness and mindfulness to help readers identify and challenge limiting beliefs and thought patterns that may be hindering their creativity.

The section also includes tips and strategies for generating and developing new ideas, such as using mind mapping or visualization techniques to explore different possibilities and connections between ideas. It may also offer guidance on selecting and implementing the most promising ideas, including tips for creating prototypes or test cases to refine and iterate on the initial concept.

Ultimately, the goal of this section is to provide readers with practical strategies for developing their creativity and innovation skills, as well as the confidence and motivation to apply these skills in their personal and professional lives. By cultivating these skills, readers are better equipped to adapt to changing circumstances, identify new opportunities, and find innovative solutions to complex problems.

The final section of the book, **"Applying Creativity and Innovation,"** is designed to help readers apply the concepts and strategies learned in the previous sections to real-world situations.

The section begins by exploring how creativity and innovation can be applied in different contexts, such as personal life, business, and society. It provides examples of successful creative and innovative endeavors across different industries and sectors, including technology, healthcare, and education. By examining these examples, readers can gain a better understanding of how creativity and innovation can be leveraged to drive positive change in different areas of life.

The section then provides practical tips and strategies for implementing creative and innovative solutions in different areas of life. For example, it may offer guidance on using design thinking methodologies to develop user-centered solutions in business or social contexts, or on leveraging technology to improve personal productivity and creativity.

Additionally, the section may include case studies or success stories of individuals or organizations that have successfully applied creativity and innovation in different areas of life. These examples can provide inspiration and practical guidance for readers looking to apply their newfound creativity and innovation skills in their own lives.

Ultimately, the "Applying Creativity and Innovation" section aims to help readers apply the concepts and strategies learned in the previous sections to real-world situations. By doing so, readers can become more confident and effective problem solvers, innovators, and change agents in their personal and professional lives.

The book's structure is designed to be accessible and engaging for a wide range of readers. It includes clear and concise explanations of key concepts, as well as practical exercises and activities that readers can complete on their own or with others. The book also includes case studies and real-world examples to help illustrate key concepts and to inspire readers to apply their creativity and innovation skills in their own lives. Overall, the book is designed to be a comprehensive and practical guide to developing creativity and innovation skills that readers can apply in a variety of personal and professional contexts.

Understanding Creativity and Innovation

Creativity

Creativity is the ability to generate new and original ideas, concepts, or solutions that are not obvious or straightforward. It involves divergent thinking, which is the process of generating many different ideas or possibilities, followed by convergent thinking, which is the process of selecting the most promising idea and turning it into something tangible.

Creativity can manifest itself in many ways, such as art, music, literature, or scientific research. It can be spontaneous or deliberate, individual or collaborative, and can be applied to personal, social, or professional contexts. Creative individuals are often characterized by their openness to new experiences, their willingness to take risks, and their ability to see things from different perspectives.

Some examples of creativity may include,

- A painter creating a unique piece of art using new techniques and materials
- A musician composing a new piece of music that blends different genres and styles
- An author writing a novel with a new and innovative plot structure
- A scientist proposing a new hypothesis or approach to solving a research problem
- An entrepreneur developing a new business idea that disrupts the status quo.

Forms of Creativity

Creativity can take many different forms, and it can be expressed in a variety of ways. Some of the most common forms of creativity include:

Artistic creativity

Artistic creativity refers to the ability to create and express oneself through visual or performing arts. This includes a wide range of disciplines, such as painting, drawing, sculpture, photography, music, dance, and theater.

Artistic creativity involves using imagination and originality to produce works of art that are aesthetically pleasing or emotionally powerful. It often involves experimenting with different techniques and styles, as well as taking risks and pushing boundaries.

It can be a powerful form of self-expression, allowing artists to communicate their thoughts, emotions, and ideas to others. It can also be a way to explore new perspectives and ways of looking at the world.

Artistic creativity can be used to create public art that beautifies and enriches communities or to raise awareness about important social issues through artistic expression.

In fact, artistic creativity is an important form of human expression that has been a part of human culture for centuries. It continues to play an important role in shaping our society and can be a powerful force for promoting social change and individual growth.

Literary creativity

Literary creativity refers to the ability to express oneself through the written word. It includes a wide range of forms, such as poetry, fiction, non-fiction, journalism, and even social media posts and blog entries.

Literary creativity involves using imagination, originality, and language skills to craft works that are engaging, thought-provoking, or informative. It often involves exploring new ideas and perspectives, as well as experimenting with different writing styles and techniques.

Like artistic creativity, literary creativity can be a powerful form of self-expression, allowing writers to communicate their thoughts, emotions, and ideas to others. It can also be a way to connect with readers and build communities around shared interests and values.

Literary creativity can be used to raise awareness about important social issues, document historical events or cultural traditions, or inspire new ways of thinking about the world.

Scientific creativity

Scientific creativity refers to the ability to use imagination, originality, and critical thinking skills to solve scientific problems, develop new theories, and innovate in the fields of science, technology, engineering, and mathematics (STEM).

Scientific creativity involves exploring new ideas and hypotheses, designing experiments to test them, and analyzing data to draw conclusions. It often involves collaborating with others and taking risks to pursue innovative solutions to complex problems.

Scientific creativity can be a powerful tool for advancing knowledge and understanding in a wide range of fields. It can lead to new technologies and innovations that improve people's lives, as well as provide a deeper understanding of the natural world and our place in it.

Scientific creativity can be used to address pressing social issues, such as climate change or global health crises, and to promote international cooperation and understanding.

Entrepreneurial creativity

Entrepreneurial creativity refers to the ability to identify and pursue new business opportunities through innovative thinking and problem-solving. It involves using creativity and originality to develop new products, services, or business models that meet the needs of consumers or address market gaps.

It often involves taking risks, as well as collaborating with others, and seeking feedback from customers and stakeholders. It requires a willingness to challenge conventional thinking and to experiment with new ideas and approaches.

Entrepreneurial creativity can be a powerful force for economic growth and innovation. It can lead to the creation of new jobs, the development of new industries, and the advancement of technology and innovation.

It can be used to address social issues, such as poverty or inequality, and to promote social and environmental sustainability.

Social creativity

Social creativity refers to the ability to generate and implement new ideas and solutions to social problems and challenges. It involves applying creativity and innovation to address social issues such as poverty, inequality, discrimination, and social injustice.

Social creativity often involves collaboration with individuals and groups from diverse backgrounds, including community members, social activists, and policymakers. It requires an ability to think outside the box and challenge traditional approaches to social issues.

It can be a powerful force for social change and transformation. It can lead to the development of new policies and initiatives that promote social justice and equality, as well as the creation of new social movements and grassroots organizations.

Social creativity can be used to promote social inclusion and diversity, as well as to celebrate the richness and diversity of different cultures and traditions.

Personal creativity

Personal creativity refers to the ability to express oneself creatively through various forms of art, writing, music, or other forms of self-expression. It involves using one's imagination, originality, and unique perspective to create something new and meaningful.

Personal creativity is often seen as a way to express one's innermost thoughts and feelings, as well as a means of self-discovery and personal growth. It can be a powerful tool for self-expression and a means of connecting with others on a deeper level.

It can take many different forms, including writing, painting, sculpting, dancing, singing, or any other form of creative expression. It can be a solitary pursuit or involve collaboration with others.

Personal creativity can be used to challenge societal norms and conventions, as well as to promote cultural diversity and understanding.

Overall, creativity can take many different forms, and it is not limited to any specific field or discipline. Whether it is expressed through art, science, entrepreneurship, or social activism, creativity can be a powerful force for positive change and innovation.

Innovation

Innovation, on the other hand, is the process of implementing creative ideas and turning them into something that adds value to society. It involves taking risks, overcoming obstacles, and challenging existing norms and conventions. Innovation can result in the development of new products, services, technologies, or processes that improve people's lives, solve problems, or enhance the performance of organizations.

Innovation can be driven by many factors, such as technological advancements, changing consumer preferences, or market competition. It requires a combination of creativity, knowledge, skills, and resources, as well as the ability to recognize opportunities and take calculated risks. Successful innovation also requires a supportive environment that encourages experimentation, learning, and continuous improvement.

Some examples of innovation may include,

- Apple's development of the iPhone, which revolutionized the mobile phone industry and changed the way people communicate and access information
- Tesla's development of electric cars, which challenged the dominance of traditional gas-powered vehicles and helped accelerate the transition to renewable energy
- Amazon's implementation of a customer-centric business model that prioritizes convenience and fast delivery, which

transformed the retail industry and set new standards for online shopping

- Airbnb's creation of a platform that connects travelers with local hosts, which disrupted the hospitality industry and provided a new way for people to travel and experience new cultures

- Moderna and Pfizer/BioNTech's development of mRNA-based vaccines for COVID-19, which represents a new approach to vaccine development and has the potential to transform the way we prevent and treat infectious diseases.

Forms of Innovation

There are many different forms of innovation, which can be broadly categorized into the following types:

Technological Innovation

Technological innovation is the development of new or improved technologies that enhance the way products are designed, produced, or delivered. This type of innovation is often associated with advances in science, engineering, and technology, and can lead to significant improvements in productivity, efficiency, and performance.

Examples of technological innovation include the development of new materials, such as lightweight metals or advanced polymers, which can be used to create stronger, lighter, and more durable products. Technological innovation can also involve the creation of new software or computer systems that can automate tasks, enhance data processing, or improve communication.

In some cases, technological innovation can create entirely new industries, such as the development of the Internet and the subsequent growth of the digital economy. It can also lead to the disruption of existing industries, as companies adopt new technologies and business models that better meet the needs of customers and improve their competitive position.

Business Model Innovation

Business model innovation is the process of creating new or improved business models that better meet the needs of customers and improve a company's competitive position in the market. This type of innovation can involve changes to a company's pricing, distribution, marketing, or customer service strategies, and may also involve the adoption of new technologies or the development of new partnerships or collaborations.

Examples of business model innovation include the development of new subscription-based models, such as those used by streaming services like Netflix and Spotify, which allow customers to access a wide range of content for a monthly fee. Business model innovation can also involve the creation of new marketplaces, such as Airbnb, which disrupts traditional hotel markets by allowing individuals to rent out their homes to travelers.

Business model innovation can help companies to better meet the changing needs of customers and adapt to new market conditions, thereby improving their competitive position and profitability. However, it can also be challenging, as it often involves significant changes to a company's operations and may require substantial investments in new technology or marketing strategies.

Social Innovation

Social innovation refers to the development of new or improved solutions to social or environmental challenges, such as poverty, inequality, climate change, or access to healthcare. This type of innovation typically involves collaboration between different stakeholders, including individuals, organizations, and governments, and may draw on a range of disciplines and approaches, including technology, design thinking, and social entrepreneurship.

Examples of social innovation include the development of new models for delivering healthcare to underserved communities, such as telemedicine or mobile clinics. Social innovation can also involve the creation of new financial mechanisms or funding models, such as impact investing or social impact bonds, which aim to generate both financial returns and social or environmental benefits.

Social innovation is important because it can help to address some of the most pressing challenges facing societies today, while also creating new opportunities for economic growth and social progress.

It can also foster collaboration and community engagement, and help to build more resilient and sustainable societies.

However, social innovation can be challenging, as it often involves navigating complex social and political dynamics, and may require significant investments in research and development. It also requires a commitment to social and environmental goals, and a willingness to work collaboratively with others to achieve shared objectives.

Design Innovation

Design innovation refers to the use of design thinking and methods to create new or improved products, services, or experiences. This type of innovation often involves a deep understanding of user needs and preferences, as well as a focus on aesthetics, functionality, and usability.

Examples of design innovation include the development of new products or services that incorporate novel or innovative features, such as the first iPod or the Tesla electric car. Design innovation can also involve the redesign of existing products or services to better meet the needs of users, such as the redesign of public spaces to be more accessible or user-friendly.

Design innovation is important because it can help to create products and services that are more appealing, engaging, and useful to users. It can also help to differentiate products and services in crowded markets and can lead to increased customer loyalty and satisfaction.

However, design innovation can be challenging, as it often requires a deep understanding of user needs and preferences, as well as the ability to think creatively and outside the box. It may also require significant investments in research and development, and a willingness to take risks and experiment with new ideas and approaches.

Process Innovation

Process innovation refers to the development of new or improved methods, systems, or procedures for producing goods or delivering services. This type of innovation often involves the application of new technologies or management practices to existing processes, with the aim of increasing efficiency, reducing costs, or improving quality.

Examples of process innovation include the use of automation or artificial intelligence to streamline manufacturing or service delivery processes or the adoption of new management practices such as lean manufacturing or agile project management. Process innovation can also involve the redesign of the supply chain or logistics systems to improve efficiency or reduce waste.

Process innovation is important because it can help organizations to stay competitive in rapidly changing markets, and respond more effectively to customer needs and preferences. It can also help to increase productivity, reduce costs, and improve the quality of products and services.

However, process innovation can be challenging, as it often requires significant investments in technology or organizational change, and may require a deep understanding of complex systems and processes. It may also require a willingness to experiment and take risks and learn from failures and mistakes.

Overall, innovation is a critical driver of economic growth and social progress, and these different types of innovation play a vital role in driving change and creating value in different areas of society.

Benefits of Creativity and Innovation

The benefits of creativity and innovation are numerous, both in personal and professional contexts. Here are some of the key benefits:

Increased problem-solving abilities

One of the key benefits of creativity and innovation is the increased problem-solving abilities that they offer. By encouraging individuals to approach problems from new and different perspectives, creativity and innovation can help generate a wider range of potential solutions, leading to better outcomes and more effective problem-solving.

For example, in a business context, a company that fosters a culture of creativity and innovation can better address challenges related to product development, marketing, and customer service. By encouraging employees to think outside the box and explore new ideas and approaches, companies can develop more effective strategies for meeting customer needs and achieving business objectives.

Similarly, in personal contexts, creativity and innovation can help individuals to overcome challenges and obstacles that they may face in their personal and professional lives. By adopting a mindset that is open to new ideas and approaches, individuals can develop more effective strategies for achieving their goals and overcoming obstacles, leading to greater success and fulfillment in their personal and professional lives.

Enhanced competitiveness

Another key benefit of creativity and innovation is the enhanced competitiveness they can bring to individuals and organizations. By fostering new and unique ideas, creativity and innovation can help individuals and organizations stand out in a crowded market, leading to increased brand recognition and customer loyalty.

For example, companies that introduce innovative products or services to the market are often able to gain a competitive advantage over their competitors. By offering something that is different from what is currently available, they can attract new customers and retain existing ones, leading to increased revenue and market share.

Similarly, individuals who are able to approach problems from a creative and innovative perspective are often better positioned to succeed in their personal and professional lives. By demonstrating an ability to think outside the box and come up with unique solutions, they can differentiate themselves from others and stand out in a crowded job market, leading to increased opportunities for career advancement and personal success.

Improved efficiency and productivity

Another important benefit of creativity and innovation is improved efficiency and productivity. By encouraging individuals to think creatively and challenge conventional approaches, new and more efficient methods of accomplishing tasks can be discovered.

For instance, in a business setting, introducing innovative processes and tools can lead to streamlined operations and increased productivity. By exploring new and innovative technologies and processes, companies can reduce costs, improve quality, and increase output.

In personal contexts, creativity and innovation can also improve efficiency and productivity. By thinking creatively, individuals can develop more effective ways of managing their time, organizing their tasks, and achieving their goals. For example, by using new apps or productivity tools, individuals can automate tasks or reduce the time required to accomplish them.

Enhanced customer satisfaction

Creativity and innovation can also lead to enhanced customer satisfaction, which is essential for individuals and organizations that seek to build long-term relationships with their customers.

When individuals or organizations offer something new and unique, it can capture the attention and interest of potential customers. By meeting their needs and wants in a way that has not been done before, they can create a positive and memorable experience for the customer, leading to increased customer satisfaction.

Moreover, creativity and innovation can help individuals and organizations to stay attuned to changing customer needs and preferences. By continuously exploring new and innovative ideas, individuals and organizations can identify emerging trends and adapt their products and services to meet evolving customer needs.

For instance, a company that introduces a new and innovative product that better meets the needs of its customers can earn customer loyalty, and repeat business. Similarly, an individual who can approach a problem from a creative and innovative perspective can develop unique solutions that meet the needs of their clients or customers, leading to enhanced customer satisfaction and a positive reputation.

Increased revenue and profitability

Another significant benefit of creativity and innovation is the potential to increase revenue and profitability for individuals and organizations. By introducing new and innovative products or services, organizations can attract new customers and retain existing ones, leading to increased sales and revenue.

Moreover, creativity and innovation can help individuals and organizations to differentiate themselves from their competitors. By offering something unique and different, they can stand out in the market and attract customers who are looking for something new and fresh.

Innovation can also help individuals and organizations to improve their efficiency and effectiveness, leading to cost savings and increased profitability. By finding new and innovative ways to do things, they can streamline their processes, reduce waste, and increase productivity, ultimately leading to higher profits.

For example, a company that introduces a new and innovative product can increase its revenue and profitability, especially if the product fills a gap in the market or solves a particular problem. Similarly, an individual who uses creative and innovative strategies to grow their business or increase their income can enjoy increased revenue and profitability.

Enhanced personal growth

Another important benefit of creativity and innovation is the potential for enhanced personal growth. When individuals engage in creative activities or innovative thinking, they often learn new skills and develop new perspectives, which can lead to personal growth and self-discovery.

For example, an individual who takes up painting or writing as a hobby may discover new talents and interests, which can boost their confidence and self-esteem. Similarly, an entrepreneur who successfully launches a new and innovative business may gain a sense of accomplishment and fulfillment that can contribute to their personal growth and well-being.

Furthermore, engaging in creative activities and innovative thinking can help individuals to develop problem-solving skills, resilience, and adaptability, which are important traits for personal growth and success. By learning how to think outside the box and approach challenges in new and innovative ways, individuals can become more confident and capable, leading to personal growth and development.

Improved social welfare

Another important benefit of creativity and innovation is the potential for improved social welfare. Innovations in technology, medicine, and other areas can lead to significant improvements in people's quality of life, while social innovation can address pressing societal challenges such as poverty, inequality, and climate change.

For example, medical innovations such as vaccines and new treatments can improve health outcomes and reduce suffering for millions of people around the world. Technological innovations such as renewable energy and energy-efficient buildings can help reduce greenhouse gas emissions and mitigate the impacts of climate change. Social innovations such as microfinance and community development programs can empower disadvantaged individuals and communities to improve their economic and social well-being.

In addition, creativity and innovation can also contribute to cultural enrichment and promote diversity, which can enhance social welfare by fostering greater understanding and appreciation among people from different backgrounds.

Overall, creativity and innovation are important drivers of personal and professional success and offer numerous benefits to individuals and organizations alike. By cultivating these skills and adopting a mindset that is open to new ideas and approaches, individuals and organizations can enhance their ability to achieve their goals and make a positive impact on the world around them.

Obstacles that can Hinder the Creative Process

There are several obstacles that can hinder the creative process and prevent individuals or organizations from achieving their full creative potential. Some of these obstacles include:

Fear and self-doubt: Many people are afraid of failure or criticism, which can lead to self-doubt and inhibit their ability to take risks and try new things.

Lack of resources: Limited time, budget, or access to necessary tools and materials can hinder the creative process.

Lack of motivation: Without a clear sense of purpose or direction, it can be difficult to generate new ideas or push through creative blocks.

Resistance to change: Resistance to new ideas or approaches can hinder innovation and prevent individuals or organizations from adapting to changing circumstances.

Groupthink: Groupthink occurs when individuals prioritize group consensus over individual creativity and critical thinking, leading to conformity and a lack of diverse perspectives.

Lack of diversity: Lack of diversity in thought, experience, or background can limit the range of ideas generated and inhibit innovation.

Overthinking: Overthinking and analysis paralysis can lead to a lack of action or a reluctance to take risks.

Understanding and overcoming these obstacles is essential for cultivating creativity and innovation. By identifying and addressing these barriers, individuals and organizations can unlock their creative potential and achieve greater success.

Importance of Creativity and Innovation

Creativity and innovation are key components of personal and professional success. Creativity is the ability to generate new and original ideas, while innovation is the process of implementing those ideas in a way that creates value. Both creativity and innovation are essential for solving problems, overcoming challenges, and achieving success in a variety of areas.

In personal life, creativity and innovation can help us find new and effective solutions to everyday challenges. For example, a person might use creative problem-solving skills to find a new way to organize their time or to improve their financial situation. Creativity can also enhance personal relationships, such as by coming up with unique gift ideas or planning exciting and memorable experiences with friends and family. Overall, cultivating creativity and innovation in personal life can lead to a greater sense of fulfillment, happiness, and satisfaction.

In professional life, creativity and innovation are essential for staying competitive and achieving success. They can lead to the development of new products, services, or processes that solve complex business problems and improve organizational performance. For example, a company might use innovative technology to improve its production process or create a new product that meets the changing needs of its customers. Creativity and innovation can also help organizations adapt to changes in the market or regulatory environment and stay ahead of their competitors.

In addition to driving personal and professional success, creativity and innovation can also contribute to social and economic development. By developing new products, services, or processes that solve important problems, organizations can create value for their customers and stakeholders and contribute to the overall progress of society. For example, innovations in healthcare, energy, and transportation have the potential to transform the way we live and work and to create new opportunities for growth and prosperity.

Overall, creativity and innovation are essential for personal and professional growth, adaptability, and fulfillment, and for making a positive impact on society. By cultivating these skills and applying them in our personal and professional lives, we can achieve greater success, overcome challenges, and contribute to the overall progress of society.

Importance of Creative and Innovative Thinking

Creative and innovative thinking are essential for innovation and problem-solving. Creative thinking refers to the ability to generate new and original ideas, while innovative thinking is the ability to explore multiple solutions or perspectives. Both are important for breaking out of traditional ways of thinking and finding novel solutions to complex problems.

Creative and innovative thinking are particularly important in today's rapidly changing world, where new challenges and opportunities constantly arise. In business, for example, companies that are able to innovate and adapt to changing market conditions are more likely to succeed than those that cling to outdated approaches. In personal life, creative and innovative thinking can help individuals overcome obstacles and achieve their goals.

In addition, creative and innovative thinking can bring numerous benefits to individuals and society as a whole. They can lead to breakthrough discoveries, new inventions, and improved quality of life. They can also foster empathy and understanding, as individuals are able to consider multiple perspectives and solutions.

By cultivating these skills, individuals and organizations can stay ahead of the curve and make meaningful contributions to the world around them.

Analyzing Elon Musk's Creative and Unconventional Approach to Business

Tesla Motors is a leading manufacturer of electric vehicles, energy storage systems, and solar products. The company was founded in 2003 by Elon Musk, who is known for his innovative and unconventional approach to business.

How did Elon Musk demonstrate creativity and innovation when founding Tesla Motors?

Elon Musk demonstrated creativity and innovation when founding Tesla Motors by recognizing a need for clean energy vehicles and developing a solution to address it. At the time, electric vehicles were not popular or widely available, and there were few options for individuals who wanted to reduce their carbon footprint. Musk saw an opportunity to disrupt the traditional automotive industry and create a sustainable alternative. He combined his knowledge of engineering, business, and renewable energy to create a company that was both innovative and socially responsible.

What are some examples of the creative and innovative solutions Tesla has developed?

Tesla has developed several creative and innovative solutions, including:

Electric vehicles: Tesla was one of the first companies to develop electric vehicles that were both functional and stylish. Its Model S sedan was the first electric car to win the Motor Trend Car of the Year award, and the Model X SUV was the first electric vehicle to receive a five-star safety rating.

Energy storage systems: Tesla's Powerwall and Powerpack products allow homeowners and businesses to store energy from solar panels or the grid for later use. This reduces reliance on fossil fuels and increases energy independence.

Supercharger network: Tesla has developed a network of fast-charging stations that allows drivers to recharge their vehicles quickly and conveniently. This has helped to alleviate concerns about "range anxiety" and make electric vehicles a more practical option for long-distance travel.

What obstacles has Tesla faced in its efforts to innovate?

Tesla has faced several obstacles in its efforts to innovate, including:

Cost: Electric vehicles are typically more expensive than gasoline-powered cars, which can make them less accessible to some consumers.

Infrastructure: The lack of charging stations and other necessary infrastructure can make it difficult for consumers to adopt electric vehicles.

Regulation: Regulations and policies related to electric vehicles and renewable energy can vary widely between states and countries, which can create challenges for companies like Tesla that operate on a global scale.

How has Tesla responded to these obstacles?

Tesla has responded to these obstacles by continuing to innovate and develop creative solutions. The company has worked to reduce the cost of its vehicles by improving production efficiency and investing in research and development. It has also invested in the expansion of its charging network and worked to educate consumers about the benefits of electric vehicles. In addition, Tesla has worked to influence policy and regulation at the local, national, and international levels, advocating for incentives and subsidies that promote clean energy and reduce carbon emissions.

Conclusion

Overall, Tesla's commitment to creativity and innovation has helped to make electric vehicles more accessible and mainstream. The company's success serves as an inspiration to other businesses and individuals who are looking to make a positive impact on the environment and society.

Cultivating Creativity and Innovation

Practical Tools and Strategies to Develop Creativity and Innovation Skills

There are various practical tools and strategies that one can use to develop creativity and innovation skills. Using these tools can be beneficial for one's personal and professional development, as well as achieving self-satisfaction.

Mind mapping

Mind mapping is a powerful tool that can be used to develop creativity and innovation skills. It is a visual technique that involves creating a diagram to represent ideas, concepts, and relationships. It is often used as a brainstorming tool, allowing individuals or teams to generate and organize ideas in a non-linear and creative way.

To create a mind map, start with a central idea or concept and then branch out to related sub-ideas or concepts. Each branch can then be further expanded to include more specific ideas or details. The resulting diagram is a visual representation of the thought process and can be used to generate new ideas, identify relationships between ideas, and organize information in a meaningful way.

Mind mapping can be used in a variety of contexts, including personal goal setting, project planning, and creative problem-solving. It is particularly effective in situations where there is a need to generate new ideas or explore multiple solutions to a problem.

To effectively use mind mapping as a tool for creativity and innovation, it is important to approach it with an open and non-judgmental mindset. Allow ideas to flow freely without censoring or criticizing them. Use color, images, and symbols to help make connections and generate new ideas.

Some tips for using mind mapping as a creativity and innovation tool include:

- Start with a clear and concise central idea or concept
- Use short phrases or keywords to represent ideas or concepts
- Use color, images, and symbols to add visual interest and help make connections
- Allow for multiple branches and sub-branches to represent different levels of detail
- Encourage free-flowing thinking without censorship or judgment
- Use the mind map as a tool to generate new ideas and explore multiple solutions to a problem.

By using mind mapping as a tool for creativity and innovation, individuals and teams can develop their ability to generate new and innovative ideas, organize information in a meaningful way, and approach problems from a fresh and creative perspective.

Brainstorming

Brainstorming is a creative technique used to generate a large number of ideas in a short amount of time. The technique involves a group of people coming together to share ideas and build upon each other's suggestions to come up with innovative solutions to a problem or challenge.

The following are some practical steps to conduct a brainstorming session:

- Define the problem or challenge: Before beginning the brainstorming session, it is essential to clearly define the problem or challenge that needs to be addressed.

- Choose a facilitator: A facilitator can help to guide the brainstorming session and ensure that everyone has an equal opportunity to share their ideas.

- Set a time limit: It is essential to set a time limit for the brainstorming session to ensure that everyone stays focused and engaged.

- Encourage wild ideas: Brainstorming is all about generating as many ideas as possible, so it is important to encourage wild and unconventional ideas.

- Build upon each other's ideas: As the brainstorming session progresses, it is important to build upon each other's ideas to come up with innovative solutions.

- Evaluate the ideas: After the brainstorming session, it is important to evaluate the ideas and select the most promising ones to further develop.

Brainstorming can be a powerful tool for developing creativity and innovation skills. It encourages participants to think outside the box and come up with new and innovative ideas.

SCAMPER

SCAMPER is a creative thinking technique that helps to generate new ideas by asking a series of questions that challenge existing products, processes, or ideas. The technique was developed by Bob Eberle and later popularized by Michael Michalko. SCAMPER stands for:

S - Substitute: What can be replaced or substituted in the idea?

C - Combine: What can be combined with the idea to make it more interesting or efficient?

A - Adapt: Can the idea be adapted to fit a different context or purpose?

M - Modify: What can be modified or changed in the idea to make it better?

P - Put to another use: How can the idea be used in a different way or for a different purpose?

E - Eliminate: What can be eliminated from the idea to make it simpler or more effective?

R - Reverse: How can the idea be reversed or turned around to create something new?

By using SCAMPER, individuals or teams can generate a variety of creative solutions to a problem or challenge. The technique helps to break down established patterns of thinking and encourages individuals to think outside the box. It can be applied in various fields, including business, education, and personal development.

To use SCAMPER, start by identifying the idea or product that you want to improve. Then, ask the SCAMPER questions, one by one, and write down any new ideas or variations that come to mind. Encourage yourself or your team to come up with as many ideas as possible, without evaluating or judging them at this stage. Once you have a list of potential solutions, you can evaluate them and select the most promising ones to develop further.

Some questions to ask when using SCAMPER:

- What can we substitute in our product/service/idea?
- What can we combine with our product/service/idea to make it better?
- How can we adapt our product/service/idea to fit different contexts or purposes?
- What can we modify or change in our product/service/idea to make it more effective?

- How can we use our product/service/idea in a different way or for a different purpose?

- What can we eliminate from our product/service/idea to simplify it or make it more efficient?

- How can we reverse our product/service/idea to create something new and innovative?

Reverse brainstorming

Reverse brainstorming is a technique used to generate new ideas by reversing the traditional brainstorming process. Instead of generating ideas for a solution to a problem, reverse brainstorming focuses on generating ideas for the problem itself. The goal is to identify potential obstacles or problems associated with the problem or situation, and then brainstorm ways to overcome or eliminate them.

The process typically involves the following steps:

- Identify the problem or situation to be addressed.

- Define the problem in detail, including potential causes and effects.

- Ask the group to brainstorm ways to make the problem worse or to create additional problems associated with the problem.

- Review the list of negative ideas generated and brainstorm ways to overcome or eliminate them.

- Identify and develop potential solutions based on the ideas generated.

For example, suppose a company is experiencing a decline in sales of a particular product. In a traditional brainstorming session, the focus might be on generating ideas for marketing or promoting the product. In reverse brainstorming, the focus would be on generating ideas for reasons why customers might not be buying the product or what factors might be contributing to the decline in sales.

Some potential benefits of using reverse brainstorming include:

- Encouraging creative thinking and a different perspective on the problem.
- Identifying potential obstacles or problems before they arise.
- Generating new and innovative ideas for overcoming obstacles or addressing the problem.

Collaboration

Collaboration is a powerful tool for developing creativity and innovation skills. When people work together, they can bring their diverse perspectives, experiences, and expertise to a problem or project, resulting in more creative and innovative solutions.

One effective strategy for collaboration is to use brainstorming sessions. During a brainstorming session, participants are encouraged to generate as many ideas as possible, without judgment or criticism. This creates an open and safe space for creative thinking and allows participants to build on each other's ideas. Another strategy is to form a diverse team that includes individuals with different backgrounds, skills, and perspectives. This can help to generate more creative solutions and prevent groupthink.

Collaboration can also be facilitated through the use of technology, such as collaboration software, virtual whiteboards, and video conferencing. These tools allow teams to work together remotely and in real time, which can be especially valuable in today's global and virtual workplace.

Continuous learning

Continuous learning is an essential tool for developing creativity and innovation skills. It involves consistently seeking out new knowledge, experiences, and perspectives to broaden one's understanding and inspire new ideas. This can be done through various means such as attending workshops and conferences, taking courses, reading books and articles, and engaging in conversations with people from diverse backgrounds.

Continuous learning is critical because it helps individuals stay up-to-date with the latest trends and developments in their field of interest, which is essential for generating innovative ideas. Additionally, continuous learning promotes open-mindedness and the ability to think critically and creatively, both of which are essential for innovation. By continuously learning and exploring new areas, individuals can build a strong foundation of knowledge and skills, enabling them to generate more innovative and impactful ideas.

Moreover, continuous learning is not only beneficial for individuals but also for organizations. It enables organizations to stay competitive in the fast-changing marketplace and encourages employees to develop new and innovative solutions to existing problems. By investing in continuous learning and development, organizations can create a culture of innovation and creativity that fosters growth and success.

Overall, developing creativity and innovation skills requires practice and persistence. By using these tools and strategies, individuals can develop a mindset that is open to new ideas and approaches, and learn to generate and implement innovative solutions to challenges and problems.

Practice Exercises for Developing Creativity and Innovative Skills

Exercise 1: Brainstorming

Choose a topic or problem to brainstorm about. For example, you might choose a problem you're facing in your personal life or a challenge your business is currently facing.

- Gather a group of people to brainstorm with. It's important to have a diverse group with different perspectives and experiences.
- Set a time limit for the brainstorming session, such as 20-30 minutes.
- Start by stating the problem or topic, and then have each person in the group contribute their ideas. Encourage everyone to speak up and share their thoughts, no matter how small or seemingly insignificant.
- Write down all ideas on a whiteboard or a large sheet of paper where everyone can see them. This helps to keep the ideas organized and visible.
- Once everyone has had a chance to share their ideas, start to group similar ideas together and eliminate duplicates.
- Discuss each idea in more detail and evaluate its feasibility and potential impact.
- Choose the best ideas to move forward with and create an action plan to implement them.

- Follow up on the action plan and track progress toward achieving the desired outcomes.

***Remember, the goal of brainstorming is to generate as many ideas as possible, without judgment or criticism. Encourage creativity and unconventional thinking, and don't be afraid to take risks or suggest ideas that might seem crazy at first. The more ideas you generate, the more likely you are to come up with innovative solutions.*

Exercise 2: SCAMPER

- Choose an existing product or service that you are familiar with. It could be something as simple as a pen or as complex as a software application.
- Write the word "SCAMPER" vertically down the left side of a piece of paper, leaving space next to each letter for notes.
- Use the SCAMPER technique to generate new ideas for improving or innovating the product or service, by asking the following questions:

  S: Can you substitute any of the components or materials with something else?

  C: Can you combine this product or service with another to create something new?

  A: Can you adapt or modify the product or service to better suit a different context or purpose?

M: Can you magnify or scale up any of the features or elements to make the product or service more effective?

P: Can you simplify or reduce any of the features or elements to make the product or service more user-friendly or accessible?

E: Can you eliminate or remove any of the features or elements that are unnecessary or hindering the product or service?

R: Can you reverse or flip any of the features or elements to create something new or different?

- Jot down any ideas that come to mind for each letter of SCAMPER.
- Review your ideas and identify the most promising ones. Consider which ideas are most feasible to implement, and which have the potential to add the most value to the product or service.
- Choose one or two ideas to further develop and test, and see how they might improve the product or service in practice.

***Remember, the goal of SCAMPER is to stimulate your creative thinking and generate new ideas for improving or innovating a product or service. Don't be afraid to think outside the box and experiment with different combinations of the SCAMPER questions.*

Exercise 3: Continuous Learning

- Identify a topic that you would like to learn more about. This could be related to your personal interests or professional goals.
- Conduct research on the topic using a variety of sources such as books, articles, podcasts, or online courses.
- Take notes on the information you find and organize them in a way that makes sense to you. You could use a notebook, a digital note-taking tool, or create an outline.
- Reflect on what you have learned so far and identify any areas where you still have questions or gaps in your understanding.
- Seek out additional resources or opportunities for learning, such as attending a webinar, connecting with an expert in the field, or participating in a discussion group.
- Apply what you have learned to your personal or professional life. This could involve experimenting with a new skill or applying new knowledge to a project or task.
- Reflect on your learning process and evaluate your progress. What worked well? What could you do differently next time? How has your understanding of the topic evolved over time?

***Remember, continuous learning is a lifelong process, and it's important to approach it with curiosity and a growth mindset. By* *regularly seeking out new knowledge and experiences, you can stay engaged and motivated, and develop the skills you need to succeed both personally and professionally.*

Exercise 4: Mind Mapping

Topic: "Planning a vacation"

- Start with a blank piece of paper or a digital mind-mapping tool.

- Write the main topic in the center of the page and draw a circle around it: "Planning a vacation."

- Think of the different aspects that go into planning a vacation, such as the destination, budget, transportation, accommodations, activities, and food.

- Write each of these aspects as a branch coming off the center circle and connect them with lines. For example, write "Destination" on a branch and connect it to the center circle.

- Next, brainstorm subtopics for each aspect. For example, under "Destination," you could write "Beach," "City," "Mountain," etc., and draw branches for each of these subtopics.

- Continue to add subtopics and branches as ideas come to mind. You can also use symbols, images, or color coding to make the mind map more visually appealing and memorable.

- Once you have exhausted all your ideas, review the mind map and look for connections and patterns. Use the mind map as a reference when planning your actual vacation.

*** Remember to let your thoughts flow freely without judgment or criticism, and to use colors, symbols, and images to enhance your map. Don't worry about making it perfect, as the goal is to generate ideas and connections. With practice, mind mapping can become a valuable tool for generating and organizing your creative ideas.*

Case Analysis: John's Great Success

John is a mid-level manager in a large corporation. He is responsible for overseeing the production of a popular consumer product, and his team has been struggling to come up with new ideas to improve the product and stay ahead of the competition. John is aware that creativity and innovation are essential for the success of his team, but he is not sure how to cultivate these skills among his team members.

To address this challenge, John decides to attend a workshop on creativity and innovation. At the workshop, he learns about various tools and techniques for developing these skills, including mind mapping, brainstorming, and SCAMPER. He also learns about the importance of creating an environment that encourages creativity and innovation, such as providing opportunities for continuous learning and collaboration.

John brings back these insights to his team and decides to organize a brainstorming session to generate new ideas for the product. He uses mind mapping to visualize the different aspects of the product and identify potential areas for improvement. During the brainstorming session, he encourages his team members to think outside the box and come up with unconventional ideas.

One of his team members suggests a new feature that would make the product more user-friendly, and another proposes a new marketing strategy to target a different demographic. John writes down all the ideas on a whiteboard and uses SCAMPER to analyze each idea and identify opportunities for improvement.

After the brainstorming session, John and his team analyze the ideas and choose the most promising ones to implement. They start working on developing the new features and testing the new marketing strategy. Through collaboration and continuous learning, they are able to successfully implement these new ideas and improve the product.

Questions:

1. What was the challenge that John was facing with his team?
2. What did John do to address the challenge?
3. What tools and techniques did John learn at the creativity and innovation workshop?
4. How did John use mind mapping and brainstorming to generate new ideas?
5. How did John encourage his team to think outside the box?
6. How did John and his team analyze the ideas generated during the brainstorming session?
7. How did John and his team successfully implement the new ideas?
8. What lessons can be learned from this case study?

Applying Creativity and Innovation

Practical Application of Creativity and Innovation

Creativity and innovation can be applied in various contexts, including personal life, business, and society.

Application in Personal Life

Creativity and innovation can be applied to achieve personal goals and improve overall well-being. Personal creativity and innovation can manifest in various ways, such as finding new solutions to personal problems, exploring new hobbies and interests, and improving personal relationships.

For example, a person may use creative thinking to develop new approaches to managing their time or to find innovative solutions to a personal challenge they are facing. They may also use creative thinking to explore new hobbies or interests, such as painting or photography, which can provide a sense of fulfillment and enjoyment.

In personal relationships, creativity and innovation can be used to strengthen and improve the connection between individuals. For instance, a couple may use creative thinking to develop new ways to celebrate their anniversary, or a parent may use innovative approaches to engage with their children and strengthen their bond.

Application in Business

Applying creativity and innovation in business is essential for organizations to remain competitive and relevant in today's rapidly changing market. Creativity and innovation in business can be applied in several ways, including product development, process improvement, customer engagement, and marketing strategies.

One way creativity and innovation can be applied in business is through product development. Companies can use creative and innovative ideas to design and develop new products or to improve existing ones. This can involve using new technologies or materials, exploring new market niches, or coming up with unique features that differentiate their products from those of their competitors.

Innovation in business can also be applied to process improvement, which involves developing more efficient and effective ways of doing things. This can include streamlining supply chains, reducing waste, and implementing new production methods. Process innovation can lead to cost savings, increased productivity, and improved quality.

Customer engagement is another area where creativity and innovation can be applied in business. By using creative and innovative methods to engage with customers, companies can build stronger relationships and increase customer loyalty. This can involve using social media, mobile apps, and other digital platforms to communicate with customers, as well as creating unique experiences and events that customers will remember.

Finally, creativity and innovation can be applied in marketing strategies to create more impactful and memorable campaigns. Companies can use creative advertising techniques, social media campaigns, and other innovative methods to reach and engage with their target audience. This can involve using humor, emotion, or storytelling to create more meaningful connections with customers.

Application in Society

Applying creativity and innovation in society can have a significant impact on solving social issues and creating positive change. Social innovation is the process of developing and implementing new ideas to address social problems, and it often involves collaboration among multiple stakeholders, including governments, non-profit organizations, and private companies.

One example of applying creativity and innovation in society is the development of mobile health clinics that provide medical care to underserved communities. This initiative involves the use of technology to bring healthcare services to those who are unable to access them due to various reasons such as poverty, lack of transportation or living in remote areas. The mobile clinics can reach people in rural and hard-to-reach communities, providing them with necessary healthcare services that are critical to their well-being.

Another example is the use of social media to raise awareness and mobilize people around social issues. Social media platforms such as Twitter, Facebook, and Instagram have become powerful tools for social activism, providing a platform for people to share information, organize events and advocate for change. This has led to the development of online communities that bring people together around a shared cause, making it easier for individuals to take collective action and create positive change.

Additionally, companies are increasingly recognizing the importance of corporate social responsibility and using their resources and innovation capabilities to address social and environmental challenges. For example, a company may develop sustainable products or implement environmentally friendly manufacturing processes to reduce their carbon footprint and contribute to a cleaner and healthier environment.

Overall, creativity and innovation can be applied in various contexts to achieve a wide range of goals and objectives. By cultivating these skills, individuals and organizations can improve their ability to solve problems, achieve goals, and contribute to the betterment of society.

Examples of Successful Creative and Innovative Endeavors

There are numerous examples of successful creative and innovative endeavors across different industries and sectors. Here are a few:

Apple Inc.

Apple Inc. is a company that is widely recognized for its creative and innovative approach to business. One of its most successful products, the iPhone, revolutionized the mobile phone industry with its user-friendly interface, sleek design, and advanced features.

In addition to the iPhone, Apple has also introduced other innovative products, such as the iPad and the Apple Watch. The company's commitment to design and functionality has helped it become one of the most valuable companies in the world, with a market capitalization of over $2 trillion.

Apple's success can be attributed to its focus on innovation and creativity. The company has a culture of experimentation, where employees are encouraged to take risks and try new ideas. The company also places a strong emphasis on design, with its products known for their sleek and modern aesthetic.

Another factor contributing to Apple's success is its ability to anticipate and respond to consumer needs. The company has a strong understanding of its target market and is able to quickly develop products that meet the changing demands of consumers.

Tesla

Tesla is a company that has gained worldwide recognition for its innovative and creative approach to the production of electric vehicles. The company's founder, Elon Musk, set out to revolutionize the automotive industry by creating a sustainable future through the development of high-performance electric vehicles.

One of Tesla's most significant innovations is its battery technology, which has revolutionized the electric vehicle market by providing longer ranges and faster charging times. The company's Supercharger network, which allows drivers to charge their vehicles quickly and conveniently, has also helped to overcome one of the major obstacles to widespread electric vehicle adoption.

In addition to its battery technology, Tesla has also pioneered autonomous driving technology, which has the potential to significantly reduce the number of accidents caused by human error. The company's Autopilot system uses a combination of cameras, radar, and sensors to allow the vehicle to operate safely and efficiently without the need for human input.

Tesla's innovative approach has not been limited to its products. The company has also disrupted the traditional dealership model by selling its vehicles directly to consumers online and through its own branded stores. This approach has helped to streamline the sales process and provide customers with a more personalized experience. Airbnb: Airbnb is a company that has transformed the hospitality industry by providing a platform for people to rent out their homes to travelers. The company's innovative business model has enabled millions of people to travel more affordably and authentically.

Google

Google is an excellent example of a company that has applied creativity and innovation to revolutionize the tech industry. Founded in 1998, Google started as a search engine but quickly expanded its services to include a wide range of products and technologies such as Google Maps, Google Drive, and Google Assistant.

One of Google's most significant innovations is its approach to workplace culture and creativity. The company has created a unique work environment that fosters collaboration, experimentation, and innovation. Google's "20% time" policy allows employees to spend 20% of their work time on personal projects, which has led to the development of some of Google's most successful products, such as Gmail and Google News.

Another example of Google's creativity and innovation is the introduction of Google Glass, a wearable computer that displays information in a smartphone-like format. Although Google Glass was not a commercial success, it paved the way for other companies to develop wearable technologies. Google is also a leader in artificial intelligence, and its machine-learning algorithms power many of its products, including Google Search, Google Translate, and Google Photos.

These are just a few examples of successful creative and innovative endeavors across different industries and sectors. They demonstrate the power of creativity and innovation in driving progress and making a positive impact on society.

Tips and Tricks for Applying Creativity and Innovativeness

Here are some practical tips and strategies for implementing creative and innovative solutions in different areas of life:

Cultivate curiosity: Try to develop a curiosity about the world around you. Ask questions, explore new things, and try to find connections between seemingly unrelated things.

Be open-minded: Be open to new ideas, approaches, and perspectives. Avoid jumping to conclusions or dismissing ideas too quickly.

Embrace failure: Failure is a natural part of the creative process. Learn from your failures and use them as a stepping stone towards future success.

Collaborate with others: Collaboration can help generate new ideas, provide feedback, and offer diverse perspectives.

Take breaks: Taking breaks can help refresh your mind and avoid burnout. Give yourself time to rest, reflect, and recharge.

Keep a journal: Writing down your thoughts, ideas, and observations can help you organize your thinking and identify patterns over time.

Experiment: Try new things, explore different approaches, and experiment with different solutions. Don't be afraid to take risks.

Seek feedback: Seek feedback from others and be willing to incorporate their suggestions into your work.

Stay up-to-date: Stay up-to-date with the latest trends, technologies, and developments in your field.

Practice mindfulness: Mindfulness practices can help you stay focused, present, and aware of your thoughts and emotions, which can help you tap into your creativity.

Remember, creativity and innovation are skills that can be developed with practice and effort. By incorporating these tips and strategies into your daily life, you can cultivate your creativity and generate innovative solutions to the challenges you face.

Success Stories

Oprah Winfrey

Oprah Winfrey is a well-known media executive, talk show host, actress, producer, and philanthropist. She is widely recognized for her creativity and innovativeness in the media industry, which has led to her enormous success.

One of the ways that Oprah has demonstrated creativity and innovation is by developing her own talk show, "The Oprah Winfrey Show." The show was groundbreaking in many ways, as it tackled a variety of topics that were previously considered taboo, such as mental health, sexual abuse, and racism. Oprah also interviewed a diverse range of guests, from politicians to celebrities, and incorporated interactive elements, such as audience participation and giveaways, which helped to engage viewers.

In addition to her talk show, Oprah has also been creative and innovative in other areas of her career. For example, she founded her own television network, the Oprah Winfrey Network (OWN), which provides a platform for underrepresented voices and stories. She has also launched her own magazine, O, The Oprah Magazine, which covers a range of topics from health and wellness to culture and politics.

Furthermore, Oprah has demonstrated creativity and innovativeness in her philanthropic endeavors. She has donated millions of dollars to various causes, including education, healthcare, and disaster relief. She has also created her own philanthropic organizations, such as the Oprah Winfrey Leadership Academy for

Girls in South Africa, which provides education and support to young women from disadvantaged backgrounds.

Mark Zuckerberg

Mark Zuckerberg is a well-known entrepreneur and innovator who co-founded the social networking site Facebook in 2004. He is known for his creative thinking and ability to innovate in the technology industry.

One example of Zuckerberg's innovation is the introduction of the Facebook News Feed in 2006. This feature allowed users to see updates from their friends and pages they follow in a single, constantly updating stream. The News Feed became a defining feature of Facebook and helped drive its rapid growth.

Zuckerberg's creativity and innovation have also been evident in his efforts to expand Facebook's reach beyond just a social networking site. For example, he launched the Internet.org initiative in 2013, aimed at providing free access to basic internet services in developing countries. This initiative later evolved into the Free Basics program, which provided free access to selected websites and services.

Another example of Zuckerberg's innovation is his development of virtual reality technology through Facebook's acquisition of Oculus VR in 2014. Zuckerberg has stated his belief that virtual reality has the potential to transform how people communicate and interact, and Facebook has been investing heavily in the technology in recent years.

Zuckerberg's success in innovating and building Facebook into one of the most influential companies in the world has made him a role model for aspiring entrepreneurs and innovators. His ability to think creatively and take risks has been key to his success and serves as an inspiration to others looking to make their mark on the world.

J.K.Rowling

J.K. Rowling is a British author who is best known for her bestselling Harry Potter series. She is a great example of someone who has applied creativity and innovativeness in her work and achieved remarkable success.

Rowling came up with the idea for Harry Potter while she was on a delayed train from Manchester to London in 1990. The idea came to her fully formed and she spent the next five years writing the first book in the series, Harry Potter and the Philosopher's Stone. It was rejected by several publishers before finally being accepted by Bloomsbury in 1997. The book was an instant success and went on to become a global phenomenon, with over 500 million copies sold worldwide.

Rowling's success can be attributed to her creative imagination and her ability to think outside the box. She created a rich and complex world full of magical creatures, spells, and characters that captured the imaginations of readers young and old. Her innovative use of social media also played a key role in the success of the Harry Potter franchise. She was one of the first authors to embrace social media, using platforms like Twitter to engage with her fans and keep them up to date on the latest developments in the series.

Rowling's success is a testament to the power of creativity and innovativeness. She was able to create a world that people around the world fell in love with, and she did so by thinking creatively and outside the box. Her ability to connect with fans through social media also helped to create a loyal and engaged community around the Harry Potter franchise.

www.ingramcontent.com/pod-product-compliance
Lightning Source LLC
Chambersburg PA
CBHW051912250726
48659CB00002B/610